Rainbow Living

Rainbow Living

A Journey Begins

Tracey A. Rockey

authorHOUSE®

AuthorHouse™ UK Ltd.
1663 Liberty Drive
Bloomington, IN 47403 USA
www.authorhouse.co.uk
Phone: 0800.197.4150

Scripture taken from *The Message: The bible in contemporary language*.
© NavPress Publishing Group, 1993, 1994, 1995, 1996.

Published by AuthorHouse 10/17/2014

ISBN: 978-1-4969-8979-6 (sc)
ISBN: 978-1-4969-8980-2 (hc)
ISBN: 978-1-4969-8981-9 (e)

Contents

Introduction

Rainbows, for some, are about wishful thinking – a pot of gold, a pleasant experience. It is a spectacular effect as the sunshine reflects and refracts the spectrum of colours across the sky. However, in the Bible the rainbow was a sign that God put in the sky in order to remind people that He is a God who keeps his promises; it was a clear statement of His faithfulness to and overwhelming love for His people. God promised Noah and his family that they would be safe from the flood. The flood would destroy those who refused to turn from their selfish ways, those who had spent their lives striving to achieve for their own gain, rather than nurturing and sustaining the creation which He had given for their pleasure. God protected Noah's family from the destructive forces that obliterated so much. Even though they had to hold fast to the hope that God's promise would be fulfilled they did not give up, they faced ridicule and were ostracised by those around them, yet they continued to believe. This hope and this faith was rewarded, a sign was given to seal that promise: a covenant of His eternal love, the rainbow.

When all is well it is easy to daydream – to imagine how we may spend the gold we find in that pot at the end of a rainbow, to think about 'wishes' we would like to see become realities given the opportunity. For some, the lives they live appear to be a somewhat "charmed" existence: everything falling into place at the right time – a fulfilling job, an ideal partner, a dream home, great health, and a perfect family, and we may find ourselves somewhat envious of such people. However, there comes a time when all lives are challenged: when you find your values, your hopes, and even your faith shaken to its very core.

The response to such challenges is what makes the Rainbow story one worthy of your attention. Many lives that appear at first glance to be very much in control – to be like that graceful swan gliding across the water, when turned upside down reveal feet that are paddling for all they are worth to keep themselves on course. The challenges of life can cause pain and frustration, and they may result in anxiety and tears, but those who share their story in this book have clung on to God's faithfulness. God is their hope and protector; it is His constancy that keeps them going through the darkest of nights.

Visit the Rainbow House, and you will be greeted by special people. Each young person who lives there has his or her own specific needs. They could only ever have dreamed of a life lived independently of their families. You would not expect to meet them in their own home, supported by Christian carers, and if you ever have the chance to visit, it truly is their home – nothing could be further from the feel of an institution than this place. Against the odds, despite living in a society that is sometimes reluctant to recognise the potential of young people with special needs, for these young people their dream has been realised. Their parents began the fight for them – some even before they were born. As families they have held on to God's promises and trusted God, continuing to believe when others doubted, or even turned away.

Welcome to Rainbow Living, a charity that enables these young people to live full and productive lives, based on Christian principles, by providing them with accommodation. They share a common faith and a home together. They laugh and cry, and they deal with the challenges that life throws at them, supported and enabled by carers and a care provider. It has been a privilege to share in their story, and we hope that you will be inspired as you see for yourselves what incredible things can happen when you trust God and allow His faithfulness to win through. My thanks go to the young people, their families, and those involved in their support and care for allowing me an insight into their lives, which in turn is shared here with you.

Names have been changed in the production of this book in order to protect the privacy of those whose stories are included; the events as recorded are real.

"Our Home": mosaic created by young people living at Rainbow House.

Psalm 103

God makes everything come out right;
he puts victims back on their feet.
He showed Moses how he went about his work,
opened up his plans to all Israel.
God is sheer mercy and grace;
not easily angered, he's rich in love.
He doesn't endlessly nag and scold,
nor hold grudges forever.
He doesn't treat us as our sins deserve,
nor pay us back in full for all our wrongs.
As high as heaven is over the earth,
so strong is his love to those who fear him.
As far as the sunrise is from the sunset,
he has separated us from our sins.
As parents feel for their children,
God feels for those who fear him.
He knows us inside and out,
keeps in mind that we are made of mud.
Men and women don't live very long;
like wildflowers they spring up and blossom,
But a storm snuffs them out just as quickly,
leaving nothing to show they were here.
God's love, though, is ever and always,
eternally present to all who fear him,
Making everything right for them and their children
as they follow his Covenant ways
And remember to do whatever he said.

(Eugene H. Peterson, *The Message: The Bible in contemporary language*)

Arts and Crafts

It's Friday morning, which means that Janet will be coming to do arts and crafts. Before you even get to the front door you are greeted with the results of sessions like these; the raised beds in the front garden were produced by the young people. There is a mural beside the door, alive with scenes of flowers, ladybirds, butterflies, dragonflies, and even cows in a field – the details reflecting the interests of those who live in the house. There is an open porch surrounding the front door and on the opposite wall is the name of the house, welcoming visitors with its artful decoration of shells and flowers. All manner of creative techniques have been employed to engage the hands of the occupants and express their unique characters.

Joshua comes to the door to greet me, smiling confidently. He introduces himself, asks me a few questions: What is my name? Would I like a drink? He then talks about what he has been doing, and offers to take me up to meet his family. We head upstairs with one of the support workers where he proudly opens the door to his room. On his wall are numerous photographs, and he fills me in on who's who, including where they live and what they do - this is me and dad when we went sailing, this is me at my gran's house in Cornwall, and that is my aunty... On the opposite wall there are pictures of famous actors; he knows each one and can talk about the films that they have been in. He laughs and jokes about things he has enjoyed watching, especially what he thought was a very funny film on his latest trip to the cinema.

Back in the kitchen he gets a cup out of one of the cupboards and makes himself some tea. The cup has an image of a steam train on it, and he shares his interest in trains with me. We talk about different railways he has had the chance to make journeys on and discover that we have even been on some of the same trains.

The other lads are busy working in the garden, so we head outside to join in. The pond has become overrun with weeds, and it needs some attention. One of the carers comes outside wearing a pair of yellow plastic gloves; they are so long that they cover her whole arms. Joshua immediately offers to help out and pulls on the gloves. He jokes about how you would need them in order to help out with the cows, and everyone laughs. More hilarity follows as the excess weeds are pulled out of the pond and deposited in a bag that Jack is holding for Joshua; the weeds are dripping and splashing everybody who is at close range.

The young people encourage one another while each does his or her own part. Stephen is putting the leaf litter into the compost bins, pushing the wheelbarrow round to the bins as it gets filled up. When he has finished that job he soldiers on to clear the ground that surrounds the pond, pulling up the weeds and pruning any branches that get in the way. He is diligent and focused – he knows just what he wants. As the area is transformed he stands back to survey the scene, the smile creeping on to his face reflecting his sense of achievement. Tasks that need to be done are completed with a sense of purpose and fun. Who could have imagined a scenario such as this? These young people are not just being cared for but also supported to do those everyday tasks that any person may complete in order to maintain their home.

The girls are more often found indoors engaged in the craft work. Beautiful craft pieces are on display, and the table itself has been transformed with a mosaic that reflects the home they share together. Pictures hang on the walls – calm seascapes, and there are wall hangings made from wool. There is a fun rainbow-coloured notice board. Copper fish have been made; by cutting the copper then hammering it into shape. Each member of the household has the opportunity to express themselves in a way that reflects their character, and at the focus of it all is the faith that they share – a heart-shaped board with heart-shaped pictures of their hobbies has Jesus displayed at the centre.

Alison has gone out with her mum today, but Sarah is here, and she loves to make things. She has a real creative flair; her room is full of things she has made. She proudly shows me the various items and talks about where she made them, who helped, and which ones she particularly likes. Her face is full of excitement as she shows me the objects she created; she feels valued as people express their pleasure in her work.

Downstairs, Sarah happily follows Janet's instructions – "puffing" the glue on to the tiles that they had painted on a previous occasion, thereby creating a raised design that not only looks effective but has a pleasing texture. Her hands ever busy, she has her colouring book in her hand while music plays on the CD player. Her mind is engaged with the job. She is listening and responding to Janet, ready to contribute her thoughts. She asks for the glitter ball to be turned on, and as it spins she dances and sings along to the music. She is happy. This is her home.

Jack has come inside; he needs to have his lunch early today, as he has a hydrotherapy session scheduled. These sessions are essential to help relax his muscles and relieve the tension in his body so that he can remain flexible. Despite his physical limitations he is fully aware of the interactions that go on around him and has an incredible sense of humour. Wherever he is it is not long before you hear laughter. He certainly knows how to communicate his sense of fun.

Mural created by young people living in Rainbow House

House sign created by young people living in Rainbow House

Jack's story

Everyone seemed to be having babies.

Mark and Hannah had reached a point in their lives where they had studied hard, found a job, met that special someone, married, and become accustomed to married life. They, too, had begun to think about babies. It seemed like the next logical step for them.

Babies were clearly part of the cycle of life: school girls conceive without even wanting to, some mothers are ripe with baby number four, and yet it wasn't happening for Mark and Hannah. That's how it began: wanting to start a family but having no success. The frustration and anxiety began to build, and a sense of despondency began to creep in – would it ever happen for us?

After trying for what seemed like forever, nature seemed to be saying that this isn't going to work. What could we do? They decided to move on to the next step of seeing if the medical profession could help. There begins another journey: tests, undignified procedures, specialists examining you, and finally medication to assist nature in the process of conception. That tiny egg becomes fertilised, and joy! But fear, too, knowing it would be a long and difficult journey from here. Nothing is real until you can hold that child in your arms, feel his or her breath, and hear the cry of life.

As the pregnancy progressed it became evident that things were not going to be straightforward; instead of blooming there was monitoring, bleeding, and not enough weight gain. Why can't we just relax and enjoy the moment? People around us were kind and supportive; the church was there: a rock to stand firm on. However, there was nothing that anyone could do to deal with the problems that were coming our way. Hospital is the last place you want to be, but you will do anything to protect that life that is inside you, to allow him to grow and develop and be strong. Tears fell, and desperate prayers were uttered. "God, don't leave us now!"

The medics decided that it was time for the baby to be born. "It's too soon; there are still nine weeks of growing and developing that need to take place," we cried. The cries fell on deaf ears.

"He will be safer out of the womb." Surely it couldn't be happening. Not now. Not yet.

Against the odds Jack Robert was born on Sunday 18 November 1984. He was tiny. He was perfect. He was our firstborn son.

Whisked away, there was no moment to linger over his perfect form or to breathe in the newness of his skin. With just a brief glimpse, he was taken to the Special Care Baby Unit. What more care could a baby need than to be held close to his mother's breast? A new language needed to be grasped. Medical equipment became common place – incubator, ventilator, and medical alarms. They were all necessary for his survival. Jack needed to be kept warm; he needed to have his very breath pumped into that tiny body.

However, ventilation does not come without risks, and in keeping Jack alive the pressure began to damage his frail body. He had a brain haemorrhage. Then he had another. This child now suffered in other parts of his body, the exact extent of which was not known at the time. Swelling of the fluid around the brain – hydrocephalus – developed over a short time of being stable. At two weeks of age, there was another massive bleed. Rapid swelling led to Jack requiring neurosurgery to insert a shunt and relieve the pressure on his brain, resulting in an unusually shaped head for a time. Tiny Jack had to endure more fear, suffering, and invasive treatments. "Why can't we just take our baby home?" we silently pleaded.

With so much happening Christmas crept up on us: a time of joy, a time of expectancy, and a baby born in a stable. Fresh clean hay, perhaps? It was certainly a long way from the smell of disinfectant, interventions by medical staff, and a transfer to neurosurgery.

At nine weeks old Jack had proved he was not giving up and was allowed home. The pain and frustration continued, but at least he was in an environment that allowed space for Mark and Hannah to develop a more intimate relationship with their son. There was now no outsiders looking in – watching, monitoring, judging. However, a blockage in the shunt caused further problems; for the most part Jack couldn't feed, and what little he did manage was then vomited back up.

Gradually the information began to come, but not without a lot of searching. Jack needed the comfort of being in contact with another person. He had to be carried constantly. He continued to have problems feeding and spent hours each day crying, in distress. He needed a monitor on him at night to check he was still breathing. By ten months old he still wasn't moving as he should have been, so it was back down to the community clinic, where Jack was referred to a paediatrician. Then came a diagnosis; Jack had cerebral palsy – that was why he could not suck, found it difficult to feed, and had spasms. We were told that he wouldn't ever be able to sit, walk, or talk and that he had a visual impairment.

Devastated. This was too much to take in. "Where do we go from here? A diagnosis is surely a good thing, but what next?" A new journey began. It started with many hours of research. "What are the implications of cerebral palsy? How does it affect the sufferer? What can be done to improve their situation?" Jack was not going to be left floundering; everything would be done to improve his quality of life.

Conductive education seemed to offer hope. This is a comprehensive learning method that has been specifically developed for children and adults who have motor disorders, such as cerebral palsy. Although originating in Hungary, the principles could be used to help Jack. A conductor – a person who specialised in this system, was employed to come into the home on a part-time basis, and, with the structure provided by this experience, Jack was eventually able to, first, sit – holding on to slats with splints on his arms – and then to stand, again splinted, holding on to a ladder-back chair. By the time he was three years old he was able to sit in a small wheelchair, where he could also be fed.

Health professionals gave mixed messages; some suggested that Jack wouldn't do the things we hoped for him. Few support groups existed, and those people who we found to be in similar situations often seemed worse off or suffering raw emotion following the death of their child. It was an isolating experience, a situation partly self-created in an attempt at self-preservation – you need to be strong in order to maintain your ideals and keep your hope alive, and constant comparisons with others were odious.

Contact with the health professionals continued as the full extent of Jack's ability was explored. An appointment was arranged at Great Ormond Street Hospital for a test to establish the extent of Jack's vision. On one occasion the family had to leave home at 4.00 a.m. in order to drive to the hospital – by the time they arrived Jack was so distressed that it was not possible to carry out the test. He was a regular in-patient in hospital as his needs continued to become evident.

Jack continued to grow and eventually reached an age when the question of schooling arose. At first he was referred to a specialist school in Cardiff. However, after one year, the school requested that alternatives were sought in order to address his visual problems. It was suggested that he could be taken to a school where he could be a boarder and be "looked after". After visiting the school the family decided that it wasn't the solution that they wanted for Jack.

A review in a special education magazine gave a glowing report of a unit called St Stephen's for children with little or no sight. Here, they believe that every individual has potential, and their ethos involved each child fulfilling that potential. It was agreed by the Gwent Local Educational Authority that the school place would be funded and that Jack would be a boarder there. This was not really what the family wanted - to be torn apart across such a huge distance - so difficult issues had to be faced. The decision finally taken, after much prayer and discussion, was that Hannah would move to the south west with Jack and his younger sister in September 1990 while Mark would stay behind until he had secured employment in the area. This meant that Jack could go to school as a day pupil and the family could be together in part while the other details were put in place.

As Jack grew, his body continued to go into spasm, pulling his skeletal frame out. His hips came out of his hip joints, and he needed operations to break bones and re-set them in new positions. Despite this, Jack loved physical contact with his mum and dad, especially being carried, and this seemed to bring him comfort. He regularly woke in the night and often very early in the morning, and, as this continued, Hannah and Mark had to find ways to cope with their tiredness and the other demands that life brought. Many times when he woke in the night he would be taken into his parents' bed to try to settle him, and, as he got bigger, this meant that one of them had to move out, so a system was devised where he would earn a red star for sleeping through the night. He loved being outdoors, and many happy times were spent in a back carrier exploring the countryside of west Wales on holiday. Jack also loved stories, and he spent many hours sitting on his mum's lap listening to stories of Peter Rabbit by Beatrix Potter, laughing out loud. You could almost forget that there was anything wrong. Each night they would read the Bible together as a family and pray, thankful for another day, yet not knowing what tomorrow would bring ...

All through childhood Jack had to fight for survival; problem after problem beset him and threatened to cut short the time that his parents had to spend with him. It was a hugely challenging time, but it allowed the family to learn so much. Feeding may take an hour – time scales had to be adjusted. Jack couldn't be left alone, which meant that if either parent was at work then a carer had to stay with Jack until they returned. Therapists came to the house and worked with Jack, and the family would have respite one night a week. Priorities had to change, and while all the support brings you into contact with great people, there are moments when you long to walk into your own home and just be yourself – not have to deal with other people or the issues of the day.

As he reached his teens the medical issues lessened, and Jack had the chance to develop in other areas. His personality began to emerge, and it was evident that he had a sense of humour and understanding that brought joy to others. Underneath the difficulties was a heart that reached out. Obviously there were times of frustration as the whole family grappled with difficult questions: "Why wasn't Jack healed? Why is he in so much pain?" They had to accept that he wouldn't be doing GCSEs like other young people or going to the pub with his friends. There was a struggle to balance Jack's needs with those of his sister, including ensuring that she had the opportunities to grow and develop her talents despite the constant demands that Jack placed on their time. She had to grow up fast as she became adept in the role of a carer. This was challenging at times and impacted on her life, too.

Hannah began attending a Baptist church following the move to the south west. With Mark working away, it took a long time for things to settle. However, as a result of a conversation Hannah was invited to another church in the area. At that time the church building wasn't adapted for wheelchairs, but Hannah felt that Jack was accepted and that the people at this new church were accepting of those with special needs. It wasn't easy to get to know people, but the family decided to join, and it was there that in time they met Sally. Sally was a woman who had a heart for those with special needs, as her eldest daughter, Sarah, had struggled to be a part of the mainstream groups, and out of that struggle had come the Rainbow Group. This group provided Jack with an opportunity to be with other young people with special needs in an environment where he could build relationships and grow in his own understanding of the Christian faith.

This meeting of these youngsters with special needs was the start of long-term friendships and relationships that eventually spilled over into adult life and the concept of living with one another supported in the community.

Home Group

There is a buzz of excitement; it's Monday evening, and that is Rainbow Home Group time. The young people begin to assemble in the big front room. Joshua, quiet and pensive in the corner by the window, is drinking in the sights and sounds around him. Stephen is smiling, laughing, and chatting – comfortable with this familiar routine. Sarah is quite vociferous, speaking with Annie while watching her dad, Ben, with his guitar and waiting for her mum to arrive. She has promised to be there later and Sarah is keen that everyone should know this. Joy is encouraging the others: "Let's make space for Jack over here ..." She moves a chair and Jack is wheeled in to the space. Max is there, too, full of life, and Adam is in attendance, keen to talk about the song he sang at a festival recently. The girls seem a little more reserved. Jane and Charlotte arrive and join the others with hardly a word, but plenty of smiles; these are their friends, and they are a part of this group. Alison is encouraged to come in; she sits for a while, and then she wanders off before coming back again.

The young people share their news. Stephen, Jack, and Joshua have just come back from a holiday, and while Joshua gives an account of the route of their journey with precise detail, Stephen talks about some of the activities they enjoyed. Swimming seemed to be a positive favourite. Sarah has been swimming too, and she has been going to the gym to get fit. The conversation moves from one to another, everyone being included. It's a pleasure to observe the companionship and care they express for one another – these are special young people, each with their own challenges to overcome but capable of having a common identity.

They sing some songs together, being accompanied by Ben playing guitar and the sounds of the various percussion instruments; which are at hand for those who wish to use them. Rachel shares some thoughts based on a story from the Bible, and a craft activity follows that helps them to visualise the thoughts they have shared. They chat and help one another, talking about what is coming up for them over the next week. An upcoming appointment at the dentists seems to cause some anxiety, and so they talk about experiences at dental surgeries and give tips on how to cope. Jack decides that it is time for him to go to bed, and so, after drinks and a snack, he heads off to his room to begin his night-time routine. The others return to the front room where they are all encouraged to share their thoughts for prayer: needs, expressions of gratitude, and their love of their heavenly Father. Some pray aloud while others sit quietly; all of them are earnest in their desire to be a part of this prayer time. The evening draws to a close, some of the youngsters head off home while others go to their rooms for the night.

Sarah is excited; her mum and dad are here with her, and she knows that they will go back to their house while she will stay here in her home. She is comfortable and contented, relishing in those strong relationships, yet no longer dependent upon them – a young woman learning to stand independently.

Sarah's story

It is times like these that really test the strength of your faith.

Ben and Sally had been told that they may not be able to have children, which had made their desire to conceive all the more compelling. Grief, anger, and loss were the first feelings to come to the fore on the news, yet they both knew that they had put their lives into God's hands, and so they continued to trust Him for the future. Sally felt God speaking to her in an unmistakable way; He said that they would have a child. They continued with the routine things of life with an assurance that their desires would come into being. Sally got pregnant straight away, and the child inside her grew and developed. At about twenty weeks Sally felt that there was not much movement, but regular checks did not indicate there was anything to worry about. However, underlying problems with her uterus meant that she went into labour five weeks before the due date. The midwife in attendance with Ben and Sally at that time was a member of their church. She explained that there was concern over the baby, and the early onset of labour. Basically they would leave things for half an hour before the medical team would intervene. Twenty-eight minutes later, on Good Friday, Sarah Rachel was born.

She was tiny – only 4lb, but perfectly formed and she had a full head of hair. She was taken to the Special Care Baby Unit and placed in an incubator. To begin with Sarah was fed by tube, her blood sugar was low, and a slight jaundice meant that she needed light treatment. Sally expressed milk, which was fed to Sarah via the tube. At the very start Sarah struggled to learn how to feed, but before long she got it, and within a week mum and baby were allowed home.

Life quickly moved forward. Sarah was a quiet and well-behaved baby, and there were no real problems adapting to family life. Sarah would get distressed when her clothes were taken off and when she was bathed, but she seemed lively and made eye contact. She was slow to do some things like sitting up, but the joy of having a much wanted child outweighed any concerns about the speed of Sarah's development. At fifteen months old Sarah was sitting up but not walking, and after a holiday Sally noticed how much the other babies at the local toddler group had come on in comparison to Sarah. Ben and Sally decided to refer Sarah back to the hospital; they saw a consultant paediatrician who said that Sarah didn't have any physical problems. However, he referred them on to an assessment unit.

Sally fell apart; Ben seemed OK, and the business of work helped to take his mind off things. They weren't certain what the problem was. They wondered whether Sarah had cerebral palsy – but there was no such diagnosis.

By the age of eighteen months Sally and Sarah were attending a playgroup at the assessment unit and a regular playgroup. Sarah did not mind being left in the care of other adults. She had special boots, which she needed to help her walk. There were rounds of appointments, and a whole new world began to open up to them – a place where everyone had his or her own needs and challenges to overcome. Some people were very positive, and Sally found this a challenge in itself; she could not relate to them, as she was still struggling to come to terms with having a disabled child. There were no predictions about the future, and those involved with Sarah were careful to say where she was up to and not discuss what the possibilities may be. At such a young age people were accepting of Sarah, and she loved spending time at the development centre and doing normal family activities like swimming.

The time was approaching when Ben and Sally needed to start thinking about schooling, Sally was certain that she wanted Sarah to attend a "normal" school. With a statement already in place from the local education authority it was clear that Sarah would need one-to-one support. A pre-school advisory teacher recommended a local primary school.

Sarah was welcomed into the school, and in light of her needs she spent four happy terms there in the reception class. Sarah had been assessed as having moderate delay, but at the end of this extended time in the reception class the head teacher called

Sally in for a "chat". He was very honest and said that Sarah would probably never read or write, and a special school may be the next step – Sally and Ben needed to consider a more suitable placement for Sarah. They went to look at special schools. One was close to home, but they discovered that none of the other children in the class there spoke, and while Sarah's delay had been re-assessed as moderate to severe, communicating with her peers was important for her.

At six and a half years old Sarah was offered a place at a special school in a nearby town. She went there daily by minibus and was happy – there was lots of stimulation and many small group activities. She learnt to recognise her own name and the logos of supermarkets. Sarah could write her name with support, and she went horse riding and did trampolining. The family continued with life as any normal family would; they went on holiday as well as going shopping and swimming and on family days out. Sarah had flat feet, but she had no health issues or hospital admissions. Over time the family had grown, and Sarah had two younger sisters, both of whom had also been born early.

Sarah found it helpful to maintain a routine; she always went to bed without any fuss. However, she did need support with dressing. She could feed herself, but she could not cut her food up. She was always thankful for things and never manipulative or demanding, but allowances had to be made for her, and this situation did affect the rest of the family. It was a fine line trying to balance the needs of the other girls with those of Sarah.

She had a passion for children's TV programmes like *Thomas & Friends* and *Playdays*. Sally would record them so that they were ready to play when Sarah wanted them, and Sarah would watch these programmes over and over again, enjoying the repetition. At one stage she had a problem with her hip, and she was admitted to hospital and put in traction. Sarah had to keep still, but the TV was at the end of the ward, and there was nothing to occupy her. In the end she took her traction off and walked out of the ward. Although she was supposed to stay in hospital Sarah had made her feelings known and was allowed home to continue her recovery.

Church had always been an important part of family life. Sarah was born into the church and while she was small she fitted in fine; toddler groups and Sunday school were great – she enjoyed the music, singing songs and the various activities on offer. However, as she got older Sarah found these things more of a challenge. There was an expectation that the young people would be able to read and write, which made it difficult for Sarah to join in. Her behaviour became more challenging, and she was shadowed in the sessions by an adult. While she still attended holiday clubs and youth clubs, a pivotal incident made Ben and Sally take stock. The group was preparing for a performance, and Sally was asked not to bring Sarah along that day. Ben and Sally were hurt and angry that Sarah could not join in as the other children could.

Isolation and anger could have kept the whole family away, but God's faithfulness wasn't going to allow that. God spoke to Sally quite clearly and challenged her that she could do something about the situation. It was not without a struggle that Sally came round to the idea of the Rainbow Group – a group specifically aimed at those with special needs, with concrete learning experiences: not reading and writing but acting out stories. Ben knew that music and musical instruments would be important and that he could use his guitar and singing as another way to teach about spiritual truths. The members of the group would also need to find out about one another, so they would have news books that they could bring in and share experiences from and that could provide a focus for their prayers. Rainbow Group was not intended to replace regular Sunday School – it was believed that the youngsters still needed to be a part of the whole church – so Rainbow Group would be once a month with the children remaining in their groups for the other Sundays each month.

By now Sarah was about ten years of age, and the proposal was put to the leadership team at the church who agreed that Ben and Sally could move things forward. Following conversations with other members of the church Ben and Sally drew a team together; some people were able to help by attending the group to support individuals while others offered their support in a variety of other practical ways. The teaching materials were not readily available, so they had to be produced, too. The group began with four young people but quickly grew as more people moved to the church and wanted to be a part of such a unique experience.

The group not only benefited the young people but provided the parents of the young people with an opportunity to get to know one another. As the young people continued to grow and their needs changed, so the group adapted in order to meet their needs. At the same time, the conversations between the parents opened up as the future loomed before them with all its uncertainties. There were social events to allow the relationships to develop between the families. The group moved from its Sunday morning slot after about five years and became a "home group"; they would meet once a fortnight at a home of one of the members. Sometimes they would adapt the home-group materials used by the rest of the church; at other times they would produce their own ideas. The group learnt to pray together, and during a Youth Alpha course; where they meet to gain a fuller understanding of what it meant to be a Christian, some made commitments to God for themselves, which later resulted in several of the members being baptised. The Rainbow Group made the most of all of the opportunities that came along, and the members of the group got involved in a dance workshop, including performances by the young people at a large church in the area and in the local cathedral.

Although she was not the eldest in the group, Sarah was one of the first to face the prospect of becoming more independent. When she was seventeen years of age the family made the agonising decision that Sarah was ready to go away to one of the Mencap colleges where she would stay away from home during term time. Sally struggled to come to terms with the conflicting needs of her daughters; she wanted the best for all of them. However, what was best for Sarah did not feel like what was best for Sally, and the tears fell as she left Sarah at college – still quite young and vulnerable.

While Sarah was away at college the Rainbow Group continued. The parents began to talk more about the future, and ideas began to emerge about the possibility of some of the young members of the Rainbow Group living together. The young people knew one another, got on well with one another, and there was the consideration of the possibility that they would enjoy a more independent lifestyle. The parents seemed to agree on the basis of what they wanted for their own child. What they needed was for someone to come in and set things up for them – maybe social services would move things forward.

Of course there comes a time when experience tells you that nobody will come in, pick up your dream and make it a reality. Sarah's time at college had not been without its problems, and Sarah was assessed as being on the autistic spectrum as well during her time there. When Sarah's time at college came to an end, Ben and Sally were left to look again at Sarah's future but with the added complication that she had spent a couple of years living away from home. They knew for the Rainbow House to become a reality that it would require time and a huge effort from the families. The house had not become a reality while Sarah was at college, and as she was ready to leave it still seemed a rather distant prospect. Sarah moved into supported living in Bridgwater in Somerset, staffed by a Christian organisation called Prospects. With Sarah settled there a core group of committed parents began to take control and move things forward, as otherwise it was likely that Rainbow would only ever be a home group for youngsters with special needs.

On the farm

Wednesday morning dawns – a freezing February day. The sky is grey, and the ground is solid with frost. It is not the best day to be working outdoors perhaps, but Stephen and Joshua head off to spend the day at Stallcombe House as usual. They arrive to be greeted by the other young men who are working there that day, change into their work boots and then head straight off to their job for the first part of the morning. Stephen is working outdoors with the goats, and he is soon sweeping and shovelling in the enclosure in order to make the area clean. Another young man also assists, and Frank, a member of staff, oversees the proceedings. The goats have a liking for acorns, so Frank brings some across, and Stephen spends some time giving them out to the goats. One goat is very greedy, and there is much laughter as he tries to give the smaller goat his share with constant interruption from the larger one.

Soon it's time for a break, so the wheelbarrow, full of the dirty straw and goat droppings, is wheeled out of the enclosure; they don't want to come back and find all their hard work undone. Drinks are made in the egg room, with all of the youngsters doing their bit; Joshua fills the kettle, and another young person gets the cups. They chat, laugh at one another's little habits, and swap places like a game of musical chairs. The staff take charge of the kettle of boiling water, joining in with the banter; it's a relaxed and friendly place to be.

Back to work. Being a farm there are animals that need to be dealt with, and with the weather being so cold the water has frozen, making work even more difficult than usual. Joshua doesn't like to be out in the cold, so he's largely working inside the egg room. However, the eggs have to be collected, so he has to walk down to the field where the hens reside. The collecting baskets have numbers, and so it is clear which area the collectors need to go in. Everyone knows the work without further instruction; they go into the area, close the gate, go round to the back of the coop, open the flaps in turn, check for eggs, and place them carefully in the basket, closing each flap down as they finish that section. Some of the young people feed the hens and fill up the water troughs while they are there; fortunately the water supply hasn't frozen in this area, so the job is soon complete.

Back in the egg room and without any hesitation, Joshua washes the eggs while another person dries them and places them in the trays ready for grading. Labels are stuck on the egg boxes, and the eggs are sorted, stamped with a date and boxed up for selling. It is quite labour-intensive work, but it is done without any difficulty and with opportunities for variation, the young people taking turns at the different aspects of the work rather than being restricted to a single job.

While it's warm and dry inside the outside jobs still need to be done. Stephen is ever diligent at his tasks; he loves to be outdoors regardless of the weather conditions. He heads off to the top field where the ponies are grazing; they need to be brought to an area where the water isn't frozen so that they can drink. With the help of some of the staff, the job of putting the harnesses on the ponies begins. Each time they get close to one of the ponies, however, the ponies trot away in the opposite direction, and there is much laughter as the numerous attempts to get the harnesses on the ponies prove futile. The lady who usually works with the ponies has already finished for the day, so perseverance is needed. Eventually, after creeping around, tempting with hay, and using the element of surprise the ponies are being led out of the field by Stephen whose smile confirms his sense of achievement in the result.

cleaning animal pens on the farm

Making sure all the goats are fed

Putting the eggs in the trays for grading

At last, the ponies are harnessed!

Stephen's story

Stephen James was born on 23 February 1986, a much wanted brother for Megan and son for Kevin and Jackie. The pregnancy had progressed as expected, and the birth went according to plan. However, from the moment he was born Stephen cried a lot. It was instantly evident that he had a club foot, and so Stephen was duly taken back to the hospital – every month. Here his foot was put in plaster in order to correct the position, a procedure that was then repeated until he was nine months old. It was very stressful for Stephen as well as for the family who had to cope with a baby in a plaster cast. He didn't progress like other babies; he didn't even sit up – at the time everything being blamed on the problems with his foot. Yet underneath what they were willing to say, the family experienced a nagging doubt that something else was wrong, but there was nothing specific enough to ask for help.

At eighteen months old Stephen developed gastroenteritis, which he was unable to shake off. He ended up dehydrated, and when the doctor looked at Stephen he commented on what a "floppy" baby he was. Stephen was duly admitted to hospital, and while he was there, recovering, the paediatricians began some tests and concluded that Stephen had some sort of syndrome. Those words came as a total shock to the whole family. He soon recovered from the stomach bug and was allowed home, but Stephen was also referred to a Child Development Centre (CDC) at the hospital. Here began a seemingly endless round of hospital appointments to understand what was at the root of Stephen's difficulties.

Blood tests and genetic tests brought no specific diagnosis. At birth there had been a knot in Stephen's umbilical cord, which may or may not have played a part in Stephen's problems. Without any clear understanding of Stephen's problems and certainly no explanation as to how the difficulties arose in the first place, it was accepted that Stephen had "special needs", and life continued.

Doubts appeared as to whether Stephen would ever be able to walk, and he began attending a local assessment centre. He had to wear splints and callipers on his legs, and the family used a double buggy to move him around or carried him. His younger sister Emma had also made her entrance into the world, so the pressure on the family continued to build. Apart from the round of appointments the family was given respite in the form of playgroup sessions a couple of mornings a week. On these occasions Jackie would leave Stephen screaming and return later to find him still screaming. He continued to wear nappies, and it was clearly evident that the issues were not limited to the difficulties presented by the club foot.

In small ways progress began to reveal itself. From the age of four Stephen was allocated a place at a special school in a nearby town. He was picked up each morning at 8.00 a.m. by minibus and brought home again at about 4.30 p.m. The change of school and reaching the age of five brought a calmer period into the household. Even though the school was some distance away, Stephen seemed to settle there. At parents' evening it was noted that Stephen was "happy" and "sociable" and that he exhibited a "sense of humour". Of course he still had his stroppy moments – but what child doesn't!

Stephen's character continued to emerge. While he needed small adaptations to deal with his physical difficulties – like wheels on the dining-room chairs to help him slide the chairs in and out and handrails on both sides of the stairs – he didn't have problems when it came to relationships. A very caring nature was the part of Stephen's character that came to the fore; he showed an awareness of others and noticed small details, asking about things if there was a change. Stephen was able to recognise his own limitations, and he had habits and traits that were specific to him. He recognised that he was "different" – that he found it hard to say certain letters, but he sought alternative words if he could not say the particular one he was thinking of.

Some aspects of life seemed pretty normal. By the age of eight Stephen was beginning to walk, which meant that he could play outside with the other children. They would play on go-karts, scooters, and tractors, and Stephen was so determined he even managed to ride a bike. The other children accepted him; they looked out for him and included him. Before he could walk he would always sit in the chair by the window, watching what was going on outside, waiting for the moment when he could be a part of it. Not everything came that easily, however, and Stephen continued to need nappies up to the age of ten. This could present real issues when going out for the day or when the family was on holiday. People would stare when he was accompanied into the toilets. His limited ability to walk meant that a short distance on a level surface was the only option. Stephen also had limited interest, which meant that he was easily bored on visits. He did not learn to read or write, and, as a result, many pursuits were beyond his capabilities.

Throughout this time contact with a variety of professionals continued, although there were no support groups for the family to share the pressure with. Contact with social services proved challenging at times. Little information seemed to be readily available, and it was typically other parents who alerted the family to the things that they were entitled to – like the support offered through holiday play schemes and a supply of nappies to meet the endless demand. The hospital seemed to lack consideration for Stephen's special needs at times; things were not always explained clearly to him, and his specific needs were not always regarded alongside any medical treatment he may have to undergo.

It was in the mid-1990s, around the time that Stephen reached twelve years of age, that the family began attending a church in the city. Here they came into contact with two other families, both of whom had children – Sarah and Alison – with special needs. Stephen knew both girls from school, and Stephen's family began to feel less isolated. However, while Stephen was accepted in the church, there were no special arrangements to meet his specific needs, and he was expected to cope within the group of other young people, although he didn't feel able to. Sally, Sarah's mum, decided to address the issue, and the Rainbow Group was formed – a place where those with special needs could come together and function at their level. Activities such as music and drama were part of the programme of activities they enjoyed.

As time passed relationships between the families deepened, the children became young adults, and while he was one of the youngest members of the group, Stephen's future had to be given consideration. Although the need to make the transition into adulthood and a more independent lifestyle was some way off for Stephen, both Kevin and Jackie wholeheartedly supported the Rainbow initiative and played their part in the development of Rainbow Living.

Sports

Olympic fever has hit the country. If people aren't watching sport, they are talking about it or even getting out and doing it. Suddenly, athletes are the heroes of the day. Our focus had been drawn not only to those who have achieved elite performance in the Olympics but also to the Paralympians who have received as much acclaim, if not more – as the stories of how they have overcome their disabilities in order to compete have been told.

Joshua has just arrived at the local sports arena. It's a Thursday evening and a training night. He greets various people as he walks around the track to the place where he will meet his fellow runners. Young people and adults of all abilities are warming up in preparation for their sessions. The youngsters exchange banter, and Joshua is comfortable in his group; he talks with the others and asks who is coaching them tonight. Their coach has to finish a session with the juniors, so the group head off around the track to warm up. After just a few moments they are back, stretching and taking off the top layers of their clothing in preparation for the main session. The coach arrives to start the main part of their training. Running is Joshua's passion, and he feels at home. The floodlights are on, illuminating the track, and there are spectators in the stands, yet there is no sign of tension as Joshua follows the instructions and joins in enthusiastically.

Friday morning, and it's time for more physical activity: it's down to the leisure centre for an afternoon with ROC. These sessions are specifically for young people with special needs, and ROC Active's mission is "to empower people with a learning disability to participate in community leisure, fitness and sporting activities for their health and wellbeing". Stephen and Joshua congregate with the others in a room where pictures on the board display the options for that afternoon. They put their photos on the board with the activity that they would like to take part in. Henry is there to support them, and they all head on up to the sports hall. They have a huge soft ball and are quickly engaged in passing the ball over a volleyball net. They don't wait for any instructions; they smile and call for Henry to come and join them. More people join in, and an instructor arrives, giving the group some focus. First, she divides them into two teams and encourages them to pass the ball over the net. However, not everyone is involved, as some of the participants are clearly not feeling very confident. Quickly picking up on this the instructor begins with simpler steps; she gets the group in a line on one side of the net and passes the ball to each in turn, asking them to push the ball over the net. The instructions are clear and very precise, with demonstrations, and there is lots of praise for each participant as they try to complete an action.

Each person takes their turn, but nobody is left waiting around too long. The session culminates in a game of volleyball where they can put their skills into action.

After a short break they head back to the initial room to select a second activity. Stephen and Joshua are going to the gym. Each has an individual programme to follow, and they are shown how to use the various pieces of equipment. Both are soon walking briskly on a treadmill, with Henry between them, encouraging them. Learning disability is no barrier to achieving your goals, and for Joshua sport proves to be an essential element of his weekly routine.

Joshua's story

Philip and Sue were excited at the prospect of welcoming their second child into the world. Plans were made, and progress through the pregnancy was monitored. The bump was much smaller this time around, and Sue did worry that the baby didn't move much; their first son had been 9.5lb and very lively as he developed in the womb, this baby certainly wasn't following the same pattern. The routine scans revealed no evidence of any problems, however, so the medical team reassured the family that they should not worry. But deep down the unease remained that something wasn't quite right.

The due date arrived, along with the labour pains. Everything continued as it should through the labour until the baby's heart slowed. The room was suddenly full of medics. Sue was put on her side, and the baby was delivered without the need for intervention. However, during the birth Joshua had got filled with mucus. He was whisked away so that the mucus could be cleared out, and he spent a short time in special care before being brought back to his mum who was told, "Everything is fine."

The excitement of a new chapter began; there was a new healthy baby in the house – the potential of another bright and active child to engage with and nurture.

However, the reality was very different. Joshua couldn't feed properly; he didn't suck well. As he was constantly hungry, he screamed a lot. Sue tried everything to encourage him to feed properly, but nothing seemed to help. Advice was sought from the midwife, and Sue and Joshua were allowed home with the hope that it would perhaps be a more relaxed environment, and this may help the situation – but Joshua still wouldn't feed properly.

He got so thin that he looked emaciated and sick. Later it was established that he had a very high palate, and he couldn't gain suction – but initially that had not picked up by the medical profession. He remained underweight, so he was given non-dairy based milk in a bottle.

He began to fill out a little and was a bit more content, but, despite this move forward, Joshua continued to scream. When he was awake he was screaming, and sometimes he could go thirty-six to forty-eight hours with only an hour or two of sleep. The family was reaching exhaustion with so little sleep and a toddler to care for as well; they were sure that something must be wrong. However, nobody seemed to listen.

Sue remembers going along to a mums' group. Joshua as ever was arching his back and screaming as he was passed from mum to mum. Everyone tried to calm this difficult child, but nobody could soothe him. It was so distressing that Sue wrote off the idea of ever going to a mums' group again. She could not face the prospect of going through that experience repeatedly.

Somehow the family survived the next few months, and when Joshua was nine months old they bought him a dummy. It was against advice, but finally he could be awake without constantly crying – another step forward. He was very late at reaching his developmental milestones – lifting his head, sitting, crawling, following things with his eyes – in comparison to other children. While not dangerously so, he was still underweight, and yet still nobody listened to the family's concerns, and they felt very alone.

When Joshua was about eighteen months old his family took him to see a locum doctor at the surgery. As she watched Joshua she acknowledged that something was wrong, but any prospect of a diagnosis still evaded them. The feelings of isolation grew, as Joshua would scream or kick and later run away in any social situation; visits to the supermarket, church, and friends' houses were all very difficult. "Failure as parents" was the label they felt was written across their heads as they battled on to find support and get answers for Joshua.

The family eventually got a referral to the Child Development Centre, and Joshua attended for one afternoon each week. The staff there got him "playing" with developmental toys. A doctor spoke to Sue and said, "You do know he has a heart problem, don't you?" It was said so bluntly that Sue left the building in floods of tears, devastated. As she walked away in the pouring rain Sue looked up at the hospital building and saw what looked like an enormous hand that went right around and covered the building – a sign that someone bigger was in control.

At the Child Development Centre various medical problems that Joshua had came to light. It was acknowledged that he wasn't developing like other children. He didn't play with things; he simply passed them from hand to hand. The only toy that he wanted or valued of those he owned was a small piece of cloth. The family were told that the developmental delay indicated autistic tendencies. There were lots of things he couldn't cope with; places with crowds and noise like church and the supermarket created particular problems. He hated sudden noises; they would cause him to kick, scream, and run off. If things happened that were outside of his control like a thunderstorm, balloons, a dog barking, or a baby crying then he would scream and run and otherwise become severely distressed. Many times a quick reaction was needed in order to stop Joshua from running off and putting himself in danger; window and door locks had to be installed at home.

At two years of age Joshua was diagnosed with a subaortic stenosis. This meant that his heart was struggling to do its job. His family was told that he would need surgery. The cardiologist was very helpful; he monitored the condition and delayed surgery for as long as was possible. However, when Joshua reached the stage that he would go blue when he was running or otherwise exerting himself then the time had come to address the problem. He had now reached eight years of age. Joshua had to go to Bristol for open heart surgery. The nurses explained what he needed to do: put on a gown, go on a trolley to the theatre, and so forth. Joshua refused; instead he walked with Philip to the theatre, walking beside his own trolley, fully clothed. There he was given a pre-med before being undressed, put on the trolley, and taken in for his operation. They had to stay at the hospital for a week, which meant a week with almost no sleep for Philip and Sue who dozed with their heads on Joshua's bed in a space where there was only a chair's width between the beds of adjacent patients. Fortunately, Joshua's heart has been good since; there have been no problems. The one in five chance of a re-occurrence of the condition remains; however, he is now very active and energetic.

Schooling was the next hurdle on the agenda: where would suit Joshua? Which school could meet his specific needs? Mainstream was the preferred option for the family, and they wanted to try it, as it was so hard to accept the severity of his difficulties.

Joshua went with a full-time support assistant to the local primary school. However, it soon became evident that this would not work, and within the first term the family had to re-evaluate their decisions. They went to visit a special school in the city that caters for children with severe and profound learning disabilities; many students in attendance also had physical disabilities. Joshua's parents didn't think it was appropriate when they first visited, as it was hard to accept that although he looked so normal he needed this level of intervention. However, Joshua attended; he was happy, and so he thrived there.

By the time that Joshua had reached eight years of age Philip and Sue had done some research into autism. They saw a clinical psychologist who confirmed that Joshua was autistic. Joshua was on the autistic spectrum, with severe learning disability and a chromosome disorder. The diagnosis brought Sue some relief; it enabled her to adapt and cope with the emotional side of things and the learning disability. However, Philip, who had been the strong one as far as the physical problems were concerned, initially found this very hard to accept.

Church, which had been a central part of the family's life, had become unbearable – Joshua couldn't handle it. If the microphone shrieked he would scream and run. He also found so many people in one place to be too difficult to cope with. As a consequence, one parent would go to church while the other would take Joshua for a walk. As he got a bit older some wonderful volunteers would take him into a Sunday school group and adapt the activity to suit him. There was another special needs child in the group, but his needs were very different.

Eventually, the family decided to attend another church in the city. At first Joshua remained in the foyer and wouldn't go in, but on the second week, Tim, a lad with Down's syndrome, was being baptised, and Joshua wanted to watch. He was excited and ran forward to watch the baptism – he wanted to go in the water. After that he was able to go into church, only leaving if something unusual happened like a shrieking microphone or a song that was too loud.

Through all this time the family continued to cope alone; there was no respite offered. Despite not being offered support, the family faced the dilemma of what would happen if they did pursue help. The nature of Joshua's disability meant that changes to his routine were very traumatic for him. Disturbances would lead to days of his autism being much worse, and the level of distress made most changes just too painful to contemplate. So many things caused him stress. Philip and Sue discovered that within the system there was money available to pay for a childminder for a specific amount of time a month. By using this for school holiday cover it allowed Sue to return to work two afternoons a week, bringing a welcome change from being a full-time carer. As a carer there were strict limits on the amount that you could earn, but the chance to pursue her career and have adult contact was far more valuable than the wages she received.

Joshua was never far from Sue's thoughts, and many times the future loomed ahead with a huge question mark over it. One day as she drove towards the city centre she prayed aloud to God: "I have no idea what the future holds, and I can't cope with the pain of not knowing. Alex (Joshua's brother) is very bright; he has his own future ahead of him. I don't want him to end up being a carer for Joshua. What will happen to Joshua? He doesn't fit into any of the categories; he is autistic, yet he likes to be cuddled. He is physically very active, but he is always different from other children. Please God may at least one of us outlive him, as I can't see how he will ever cope without us."

Soon the family were introduced to Sally; they went to her home and found out about the Rainbow Group. To begin with, Philip, Sue, and Joshua all went to the group, which gathered once a fortnight. Sally and Ben would lead a Bible study with the young people while the parents would be in another room chatting. Joshua loved it; for the first time he was able to have friendships with other disabled youngsters outside of his school. The parents could build a support network by sharing their thoughts and concerns with one another while the young people were happily engaged in their own programme. Things were beginning to look more positive. The Rainbow Group parents had begun to share their thoughts about what the future may look like for their children. Philip and Sue imagined a future where Joshua could live in a home with his friends, be cared for by Christians, have lots of structured activities, and be residing in the city, so they could still spend time with him.

Wouldn't it be wonderful if these young people could all live together one day? The Rainbow Living house project had been born, and although at this stage five young people and their families had already expressed an interest Sue and Philip became involved in the project. They could see what a wonderful opportunity it was for the others even if Joshua wasn't included.

When a suitable property was found, Joshua – to the shock of all – announced to his aunty who was visiting, "We found a house, and I'm going to live with my friends." Joshua's enthusiasm wasn't to be dampened, and sure enough two weeks later one of the original five pulled out, and Joshua was offered a place in the house. Going to the new church had been a turning point;

the family felt that they completely belonged, and change was happening. There were of course practical issues to deal with, and there was concern that benefits may be withdrawn, but the way in which the issues were resolved was again more proof of God's faithfulness.

Shopping

It's about 11.30 a.m., and the Rainbow House is quiet. Most of the young people have left for their various activities. Alison has come out of the shower and is getting herself organised for the day. She is a little run down; she has some ulcers on her tongue, and they are sore, and she has a tickle in her throat that is making her cough. Nonetheless, she manages a smile as she disappears into her bedroom to get ready.

Jane is working one to one with Alison today, so time is not an issue. Alison can make choices about what she wants to wear and how the rest of the day will pan out. She has decided that she needs to go shopping in order to get something for her ulcers and some new pens. There is a list of things that the others have said they need, too, including cereal and various ingredients for that night's supper. Everything is done at Alison's pace. First, she gets out her money box and purse. Then she decides, with Jane's support, how much money she will need. They count it out and put the money in Alison's purse, the figure and other details of the planned expenditure being recorded in a book so that there is a written history of what has been done. Shopping bags are gathered up.

Alison's hair is still wet from the shower, so she goes back into the bedroom with Jane to get it dried before going outside. That accomplished, Alison then has to decide which jacket she wants to wear to go to the shops. It all takes time, but there is no pressure – just patient support and encouragement. She decides on a striped fleece, which contrasts well with the dark trousers she has on. The other essentials are gathered up: medication, her mobile phone, and a coat in case of rain. For some, this may be a ten-minute process, but with Alison's autism she needs time to make choices and express her thoughts.

The supermarket is not far from the house, and the route is one that is clearly familiar to Alison; she knows the safe places to cross the road and comments on avoiding dog mess. Although in general she says very little on the walk, Alison is clearly taking in the situation, and she responds to the comments that are made.

Once inside the shop Alison is keen to get something for her ulcers and heads straight for the pharmacy. The assistant shows her the various treatments that are available, and Jane explains the differences between them. Alison opts for a type of lozenge that will help with the pain from the ulcers and also soothe her throat. She gets out her money and pays for the item, and then she is ready to continue with the rest of the shopping.

Alison doesn't eat meat, so as she looks at the various items that she thinks she may like, she needs advice on which would be suitable. Jane patiently explains what the various packets contain, and some are immediately put back – too spicy with a sore mouth, or it has meat in it, but a considerable amount of time is given to Alison to allow her to decide what she would like to buy. She is learning – first, to make choices about what she likes to eat, and, second, to recognise packaging and the items that she enjoys. This means that the choosing gets easier as she becomes more familiar with the products on sale.

Back to the list, and the items for the others in the house are located and put in the basket. Alison recognises and finds these things with minimal help, and it is soon on to the tills and time to pay. The items for the house go through first, and Jane pays for them with money from the house purse. Then Alison's selection goes through, and she pays for them and packs them in a bag.

Its lunchtime now, and Alison enjoys eating in the cafe. She looks down the menu with Jane to see if there is something that would be suitable, bearing in mind her sore mouth. Alison opts for a bowl of chips with mayonnaise to help them slip down easily. She clearly enjoys the food, and she is quite content sitting in the cafe.

Soon it's time to head back to the house, but Alison isn't going out of the door: she's indicating towards the newspaper area of the supermarket. The pens have been completely forgotten. So it's back into that section of the shop to track down the pens. It doesn't take long to decide on the ones that she wants to purchase, but then some stamper pens - which have one end for drawing and the other for printing shapes, catch Alison's attention; she decides she would prefer to have them. Jane checks the purse to see if Alison has enough money left. With the determination that she does have enough money, it's over to the tills by the door to pay before heading back home.

All in all it was a successful outing, and Alison returns to the house pleased with the results. Although she has a house key, Alison can see that the others are back and takes delight in persistently ringing the doorbell until somebody comes out to let her in. Back inside she puts her shopping in her cupboard before going in to see some of the staff and show them her lozenges. She isn't saying much but gets her message across through gestures and a few words. Clutching her stamper pens, it's obvious what's on her agenda next.

Alison is developing her skills in independent living; she is overcoming the hurdles that her condition presents. She has come a long way, and the journey continues.

Alison's story

Daniel and Mary had been married for a couple of years, and they realised that they wanted to have a child. Eight months later, Mary found herself to be pregnant.

The pregnancy progressed normally; the scans and check-ups did not suggest any cause for concern. However, Mary's blood pressure was registering as being high towards the end of the pregnancy.

The due date arrived, but the baby did not. Mary went into hospital to be induced. At first nothing seemed to happen, but the labour finally began, and having laboured through the night Alison was born at 7.30 a.m. on 19 November 1982.

At the time of the actual birth there was a lot of people in the room and lots of activity. Daniel said something about the baby being blue and oxygen was mentioned, but the joy of this perfect new life far outweighed any concerns that may have lingered in

Daniel's and Mary's minds. The family were over the moon, and Mary's mum and sister came in to join the celebrations.

Alison was a contented baby; she was placid and happy. She steadily put on weight and was perhaps a bit on the large size. She was no problem for Daniel and Mary; she never really cried for attention or made demands. She didn't sit up, but nobody worried about this because of her size. There wasn't much eye contact, and Alison was content to be on her own, with hindsight this should have caused questions to be asked, as they were clear indicators of autism. However, at her twelve-month check the doctor said that everything was fine. Life continued with a naive oblivion to the reality of the situation.

At birth one of Alison's feet had been at a funny angle, so the family were regular attendees at the hospital for checks and physiotherapy. At sixteen months old Alison had a hospital appointment with a physiotherapist, and during the appointment the physiotherapist asked who the paediatrician covering Alison's case was. Stunned, Mary asked why she was being asked this, and she was told that it was probable that her baby would never walk or talk. Somehow, despite the shock, Mary made her way home. Once home, she broke down and cried.

Suddenly, there were appointments coming out of their ears; there were hospital appointments and appointments at the Child Development Centre. Alison still wasn't walking at this point, and while the Child Development Centre provided good support there was no clear diagnosis. The family were told that Alison had learning difficulties; there was nothing wrong – she was just slow.

The time had come to think about nurseries. A local nursery agreed to take her, but Mary had to stay with Alison. Following this, when it was time for schooling they were told that the local primary school, where Daniel and Mary assumed she would attend, wouldn't take her. As a result, Alison was moved to an Assessment Unit that was attached to another local school where she stayed for the next three years. Mary got a job there working with an autistic child and began to understand the issues involved with special needs more clearly.

By now Alison was eight years old, and it was suggested that she should go to a special school. However, because of the profound difficulties that some of the children had at the special school Mary could not see it as being appropriate for Alison. She looked at other possibilities. There was another special school in the city, but they did not feel they could meet Alison's needs. Eventually, she got a place at a special school in a nearby town. Mary hated the thought of her going to the school, but she felt that she had to accept it and go along with it. It was difficult as a parent to see her child in an environment where there were such complex needs. The realisation did gradually dawn that Alison was like some of these children, and Mary would break down and cry. It wasn't meant to be like this ...

Around this time, Daniel was working away a lot, and Mary got friendly with a family who went to a church in the city. Their children went to a club there on Fridays, so Mary and her children joined them for this and went along to the church on a Sunday, too. After about three months Daniel started to come as well. A couple of families looked out for them and were supportive of them. Mary began a new job and made friends with another lady who also went to the same church. The lady would bake cakes and give things to Mary and never asked for anything in return. She also talked about her faith. Mary saw something special in that love and care; she wanted to be like this lady.

Daniel went headlong into church. He was totally absorbed by it and focused on it. This made Mary more reluctant to be a part of things, but those friendships that she had developed kept niggling in the background; she couldn't reject church but wasn't ready to commit herself yet.

When Alison was eleven years old the family joined a group out at a retreat centre on Dartmoor. During their stay they spent some time down by the river, there was a fire at the riverside that was burning with lots of smoke, and the water in the river was rushing past. Unexpectedly, Alison had a massive fit, which resulted in her being admitted to hospital. What should have been a relaxing time with friends instead became the beginning of a new set of challenges. Alison was diagnosed with epilepsy, and a new round of consultant appointments began. She was assessed as having moderate to severe learning difficulties and sensory processing difficulties. Her speech was limited, but she would use eye contact and pointing to make her needs known.

Mary struggled on; she just had to keep things together. As a couple they were invited to go on a "Just Looking" course to find out a bit more about Christianity. By the end of that course they had both made a commitment to God. As Christians they began attending a home group where they met a couple called Kevin and Jackie. Both families went to Spring Harvest (the inter-denominational Christian conference). They would talk and walk to meetings together and gradually became good friends. They discovered that they had more in common than they had first realised: Stephen, Kevin and Jackie's son, was in the junior part of the school that Alison attended. Both young people found the regular church groups difficult and were able to become part of the Rainbow Group.

Time marched on, and before they knew it Alison was at the school leaving age. Mary and Daniel had to consider the most suitable step for Alison to take next. She was allocated a care worker, and they looked at the option of Alison attending college. For various reasons Mary and Daniel determined that this did not seem to be a viable option, and Alison herself, who was beginning to express her own feelings, resisted the idea of college.

Various things relating to Alison's diagnosis still didn't really add up. By now Mary had worked with enough young people with special needs to recognise the symptoms. She really didn't want Alison labelled so had never pushed things. However, what became evident was that a "label" for Alison's difficulties was more likely to be accompanied by help and support. Alison was still under the care of the medical team for her epilepsy, so Mary asked if she could be tested for autism. The doctor couldn't understand how Alison had reached her late teens without autism being recognised; in his opinion, Alison undoubtedly had autism. Lots of things fell in to place about her behaviour and avoidance of certain things. There had always been a lack of communication, and she didn't really like the physical contact of being hugged.

Life continued to offer its challenges; Alison was attending a centre for adults five days a week where she was exposed to bad behaviour and bad language. The family found that they needed Alison to have more and more respite care, so they considered looking for a placement – but they didn't really want her to leave home. Alison was happy at home and she didn't articulate a need to leave either.

While the young people attended the Rainbow Group the parents would regularly sit and chat. They often discussed what may happen in the future, and the idea of the Rainbow Group evolving into a supported living arrangement seemed like a possibility. Alison loved her Rainbow friends, and when people outside of her family asked her as to whether she would like to live with them then Alison would answer in the affirmative. However, she wouldn't say yes or no at home, so Mary and Daniel were still left feeling uncertain.

On the outside Mary's actions suggested that she was in agreement with the idea of the Rainbow House, but inside she was angry with God. She didn't want to talk to Him. It felt like Alison was being taken away. A bid was made on a house, and Mary looked at it thinking, "This is the house that will take my daughter away." That bid failed, but the battled raged on inside Mary. What was God trying to do to her? What was He trying to say? Fundraising activities continued, and Mary was present supporting them, but her heart felt like it was being torn apart. She talked with Kevin and Jackie, explaining how she didn't want to upset Alison by saying that she had to go to the house and equally, on her own part, she didn't want her to leave home. Each family was asked for a commitment to the house as the project progressed; Mary kept the letter for six weeks before she felt able to respond. Daniel was convinced it was the right thing for Alison to be in the house; he wanted a life with Mary and had always been there for her and the children. They had to take that final step.

As the house was renovated for the young people the families involved regularly helped out. Mary was sitting outside Jack's room one day when she realised that Alison had to have a place there: Alison was being offered a home, and it was one where she would be with her friends in a Christian environment. There was no real alternative; she couldn't stay at home any longer: she was an adult and needed to move on. As she accepted the reality, Mary felt like a burden was being lifted from her, and she began to make plans with Alison. They talked about her new home and began choosing things for her room; this would be a new beginning for them all.

A step towards independence

Rainbows began with four children who had varied disabilities; all attended a church in the city with their families. They enjoyed being with other youngsters in a Sunday school setting but found it a challenge to learn and to some extent even join in. As a response to this a special group was formed in 1996 – Rainbows.

The group met once a month initially, to interact and learn together. Later on the group moved from a Sunday morning slot at the church to Sunday teatime, meeting in the home of one of the parents from the group.

Not only did the young people learn about their faith and share in times of worship together, but they enjoyed one another's company socially, and the bonds between them strengthened. Often the parents would stay and chat together while the young people had their group time, and, as a result, friendships grew, first between the young people, but also over time between their parents. The time the families spent together, with their common bonds, led to life-long friendships and resulted in developing commitments to one another.

As time moved on the families began to consider what the future may hold for their young people as they moved into adulthood. The parents wanted an environment that would allow their young people to become independent and continue to develop their personal skills. Additionally, they all had a strong Christian faith, and their desire for their children included having an opportunity to continue to grow and develop in their own personal faith.

In 2000, while some members of the group were away at Spring Harvest (the inter-denominational Christian conference), they came into contact with a charity called Prospects. Prospects are a charity whose carers and administrators are predominantly Christian. They were at Spring Harvest running sessions aimed at people with learning and physical disabilities. It also transpired that Prospects were recognised providers of supported care to people with learning disabilities. Prospects could bring the Christian ethos into a living arrangement that the parents desired.

Someone suggested that it would be a good idea if those in the Rainbow Group wishing to do so set up home together in a supported living situation with Prospects providing the care. The seed of an idea began to grow.

By now the group had grown to five families sharing this vision. The five families met, and a wish list for a potential home was drawn up:

Building

- one house/bungalow or two houses as semi-detached properties
- six bedrooms (at least two on the ground floor), ensuring adequate sleeping accommodation for young people and one "sleep in" carer with one "waking" night staff
- bathrooms.
- one adapted for an overhead hoist system
- all bedrooms to have bath or shower facilities
- staff shower/wash facilities
- common room/lounge area
- large kitchen/dining area
- recreation room
- staff office/interview room/medication storage area
- utility room
- conservatory

Access

- wheelchair accessible
- flat site
- interior stairs with two banisters

Features

- south facing
- good size garden with easy access and greenhouse, including vegetable garden
- room for animals, for example, rabbits
- sheltered from the elements
- shed

Location

- quiet
- no startling noises
- parking for residents and staff
- accessible for staff to get to easily
- in the city

Amenities

- healthcare – near GP practice and pharmacy
- post office accessible
- on a regular bus route
- near a pub
- near a local church
- near a shop
- near a café.

The overall placement should enhance the independence of the clients.

In 2001 the group approached Prospects to see if they would be interested in a project to provide a home for members of the Rainbow Group. Prospects agreed that they would be interested in providing the care package, but importantly Prospects would not provide the actual house. The Rainbow Group would have to find a house for themselves.

Initial Preparations

Around that time a government White Paper had been published – *Valuing People: A New Strategy for Learning Disability for the 21st Century* (March 2001; Cm 5086), and the contents of this paper epitomised the type of project that the group had in mind. It seemed like the idea was becoming a real possibility. Much talk and prayer continued as parents began to take tentative steps towards their goal.

Devon Adult and Community Services were contacted. While they expressed support for the project, they pointed out that as it was a unique proposal – there had never previously been an established group of people, all with learning disabilities, wanting to live together – they needed to be satisfied that it was a genuine group and that the young people themselves were choosing to live together, and the idea was not merely rooted in the aspirations of their parents.

At the time Devon Adult and Community Services was organisationally fragmented; there were areas of responsibility determined by home addresses. In Rainbow Living's case the individuals fell into three areas, three hierarchies, and three lots of bureaucracy. Key workers or social workers had to be appointed to those individuals who did not have one. Five key workers, working across three bureaucracies, had to be managed.

A co-ordinator was appointed as a project manager, and their role involved drawing those three bureaucracies together. What followed was a gruelling four years of meetings, assessments, and planning. These key people, along with a representative from the Rainbow Living parents, began meeting on a monthly basis in order to guide the project.

Both parents and the young people themselves spent time together with their care manager so that each of the young people could be certain that the project was what they wanted for their life at this time. There were assessments and dialogue in order to ascertain each individual's need, along with the level and nature of care they required.

The government White Paper had laid out a view of how people with learning disability should be valued and given choice in their own right – "person-centred planning". The parents of the Rainbow group members received training to help them understand this process. The training reinforced the fact that a person with a learning disability is put first and that their welfare, wishes, and needs take precedence over those of their parents or carers. It was crucial that everyone understood what person-centred planning entailed. Professional advocates were also part of the process, with representatives of the advocacy service meeting with the youngsters on several occasions to confirm that they really did want to live together.

During this time members of the group had continued to look into the work of Prospects; they visited properties in Bridgwater and Burnham-On-Sea and satisfied themselves that the care provision and ethics that Prospects offered were compatible with their aspirations.

By January 2005 Devon Adult and Community Services had agreed in principle to meet the care costs of the five individuals. Prospects had agreed in principle to be the care providers.

With the care side of things progressing, the group needed to look at housing. Where would the young people live? Who would provide the house? First, they approached two local housing associations and discussed the possibility of working in partnership with them. While the discussions were useful it became evident that housing association funding would not be available to provide capital funding to purchase a house for a project like this.

The parents received some advice from a charity called Housing Options. They were able to explain various options that were available at the time: mortgages, supported living, residential living, direct payments, and housing associations. This advice proved valuable in clarifying how they may proceed.

The idea of direct payments was an attractive option; with direct payments individuals receive a direct payment to meet all their needs. A direct payments officer spoke with the parents about the scheme. Although an attractive option, it was not considered suitable, as direct payments rely on the recipient being able to manage their everyday lives. None of the five young people were able to do this, nor did any parent within the group feel that they were able to take on the task, and the idea was ultimately discounted.

The information and advice had revealed a number of options for the group to consider; however, most of the options did not offer the long-term security of tenure that the group desired. It seemed that in order to have a home where the five young people could live together, for as long as they wanted to do so, without the fear of being moved on against their will, there would need to be outright ownership of the property. Decided on as the only real option, the project entered a new phase.

Much discussion took place, and there was lots of waiting for somebody to do something. Approaches had been made to various people, but somebody needed to drive the whole project on. Prospects provided the group with details of a Christian businessman who had been involved in financing other projects with themselves. The group decided that it was worth contacting this man to seek his opinion on their own ideas. A letter was sent, and within two days of posting it they received a phone call from the man, during which he said that he was interested in supporting the project. A letter followed shortly intimating that he would be prepared to put up £250,000 on a landlord/tenant basis if the project was to go ahead.

The news was fantastic and spurred the group on. They felt that God was affirming their vision. However, in the process of researching suitable properties it quickly became evident that at that time a suitable property was going to cost about £500,000. What next? How could this shortfall be met?

Awareness of the Rainbow Project had increased over the years, and several people had completed sponsored events in order to support the project. However, this was just a drop in the ocean compared to the scale of funding that would be needed. The Rainbow Group had also increased in size and evolved from a Sunday school group to a home group for young adults who had begun meeting every fortnight and had additional social events. Time was moving on, and the young people were continuing to grow up; while progress had been made the reality of the house for the young people was still a long way off.

God's timing was not necessarily sitting comfortably with that of human desires. Our society encourages us to go out and get what we want; patience is a characteristic that seems somewhat in decline, and perseverance seems to be something that many lack. Yet they are valuable attributes in God's way of living, and this reality was becoming clear.

Prospects got in touch with the group to say that the businessman who they had previously contacted was going to be in Somerset, and he was free that afternoon if they wanted to meet him. A few quick phone calls later and three Rainbow parents were in the car heading up the motorway to Taunton. It was a further time of encouragement as it became evident that this man was a Christian entrepreneur with a heart for disadvantaged people, particularly those with learning difficulties. From his wealth of experience he was able to offer practical advice as well as expounding on the financial options he was prepared to consider. All those at the meeting were reassured that the man was genuine and that if the project was to move forward then he would have the interests of their young people foremost while keeping an eye on the business aspect of things. He suggested that in his experience things often do not happen until we step out in faith with God. The Rainbow parents were persuaded that they should step out in faith and find a suitable property for themselves.

Becoming a charity

Within a month a potential property was spotted in the local newspaper. It was an eight-bedroom residential home at the top of Clifton Hill in Exeter, the location being ideal for access to their church and well served in terms of local services. Sealed bids were invited with offers in excess of £350,000; however, the final date for bids to be submitted was only a week away. Minds were certainly concentrated, and a viewing was arranged for two days later. Inside, the building revealed itself as "institutionalised"; it was structurally sound, with communal rooms that fitted the criteria of the Rainbow Group very well. The bedrooms would need a significant number of alterations in order to suit the needs of the Rainbow Group, however, and a lift would need to be installed – alterations that would require substantial financial outlay.

The estate agents seemed somewhat perplexed by this diverse group viewing the house, and they were obviously unsure as to whether the group was serious in its intentions or even able to make a bid. Comment was passed that "the committee from the church" was back.

Following a second viewing the group convened a meeting back at one of their homes for prayer and discussion. It was decided that a bid would be submitted for £354,000. So on Friday 22 April 2005, only six days after first seeing the house, the bid was placed in the hands of the agents.

Faith does not always give you what you want, neither is it an easy path to follow and the bid was not enough. Despite believing that God, through all of the positive steps and apparent confirmation, had pushed the group towards this house it transpired that this was not the property that would be the start of the Rainbow Living project.

Time ticked on, and the search continued in the Exeter area – Beacon Lane and Birchy Barton. However, nothing fulfilled the aspirations of the group. Properties that fitted the criteria cost more than the available funds. Hope was not lost, however, and as the group pressed ahead they continued to pray for guidance and direction; if a dead end was reached then a new avenue opened up.

National and local events began to influence the direction that the group felt it was being pushed in. Homes for those with learning disability were being closed at short notice by their landlords, and this went against one of the fundamental principles the group wanted to achieve: long-term security of tenure.

It was clear that with the constant changes to central funding and policies what Rainbow Living needed was to have some control over its property and its ability to offer long-term security of tenure for the occupants in its house.

In November 2005 the decision was made for the group to establish themselves as a registered charity. As that decision was made some felt empowered; they were no longer waiting for somebody else to do something.

Rainbow Living became the name of the charity, and they engaged the services of a solicitor to help with the paperwork and advise on the right phraseology to use in compiling and submitting an application for charity status to the Charity Commission. Time was given on a voluntary basis. Officers and trustees were elected, and a board was formed, the members of which met regularly in order to provide direction for the project and delegate tasks. The aims of the charity needed to be established, and the scope of its brief needed to be determined – if it was too narrow then it would not be a viable group; if it was too broad then individual needs could easily be overlooked. It was yet another challenge, but one that could be overcome.

Meetings continued, and there was much discussion and consultation. Drafts were drawn up, each person considering with honesty and integrity the strengths, weaknesses, opportunities, and threats that such a project would entail. A statement of purpose was realised, and this provided the backbone of the application for the Charity Commission. Advice was sought in those areas where those involved lacked expertise so that the final details would be robust enough to satisfy the scrutiny of those considering the application.

An application to register as a charity may reasonably be approved in as little as six weeks, but this was not the case for Rainbow Living. There was a wait of about six months before the parents were to hear the news that they so eagerly anticipated. Finally, in September 2006, the Charity Commission approved the application, and Rainbow Living became a registered charity.

Once registered as a charity new avenues of funding became available to the group. They approached various trusts and funding streams, putting in applications to build up their capital. A local Christian Trust was able to offer the group support to the sum of £500,000, but this would be on a loan basis, and it could be looked on as a mortgage that would need to be repaid over time as the project became established.

Other aspects of the project needed the group's attention: the business plan had to be re-visited, financial policies had to be put in place, insurances had to be arranged, and data protection policies needed to be agreed. Leaflets and brochures also had to be produced, and the logo had to be finalised, as well as more detailed information needing to be produced that could be used when approaching possible funding sources. A website would also be crucial in a time of so much electronic communication. As a charity it would be necessary to hold an annual general meeting (AGM), and it would be good to have a patron. The Bishop of Exeter was approached informally, and his wife suggested that he may be willing to act as patron for Rainbow Living but informed them that a formal written letter would be necessary.

Finding a house

January 2007 meant a new year and some exciting news: a house on Barnfield Hill, Exeter was coming on to the market. The house would be marketed at £550,000; however, there was an expectation that the sale price would be in excess of £600,000.

A figure of £600,000 was more money than Rainbow Living had available, and discussion followed concerning what other funding the group could realise. They came up with an amount of £80,000 that could be "loaned" to the project from their own finances – still leaving a shortfall. An amount of £15,000 was held in the bank from fundraising, and so it was agreed that £10,000 of that could be released to allow the group to make a realistic bid. But still the sums didn't quite add up.

The group were again convinced of the potential that this particular property held, but they were left wondering about how much they could pay. Was the value and interest in the property being "talked up"? What would the added value be in terms of its size and position? Would an independent valuation indicate a significantly different price? Should they really be offering more than the £500,000 provided by the Christian Trust? Were they trying to do things in their own strength rather than relying on God?

It was agreed that it would be prudent to seek more prayer, guidance, and information. A prayer letter was sent out to the regular supporters of the Rainbow project encapsulating their dilemma:

> The group still feels that the property ticks all the boxes. Its size and location would be hard to better but we haven't got an open cheque book and in any event it would be irresponsible of us and a poor example of stewardship if we paid over the odds for the property.

> The Trust is still committed to us and we are able to raise some additional monies to those pledged by the trust. The fact that we can raise some additional money has raised the question of whether we are straying into the area of trying to do things in our own strength and not trusting God to provide for our needs.

> The big prayer request is that we get much needed guidance and wisdom to make an offer that will not only secure the house but still leave us sufficient funds to make the alterations and décor changes it needs to meet our needs.

Alongside the prayer came action, and while they waited on God they used the skills God had given them to look at the house in more detail. It was ascertained that the Trust was agreeable to Rainbow Living proceeding without a full structural survey but that one would need to take place prior to completion on the property. An asbestos survey was undertaken, as was an electrical survey. A refurbishment plan was made, and potential costings for the work were compiled. Planning consents and change of use were checked. Finally, it was agreed that Rainbow Living would offer £561,000 for the Barnfield Hill property.

The vendors had invited sealed bids, and the highest bid would be the one that was accepted. The date for bids came and passed, and the feelings of hope were short lived; the property had been purchased for office development. There had been both higher and lower bids than theirs, but yet again Rainbow Living seemed to be getting an answer from God, and that answer was a resounding *no*.

Down but not out, the group felt that they had been good stewards of the funds that were available to them and that the bid had been correct at that time, and further discussion ensued regarding the best strategy to adopt in the light of events. These discussions confirmed once again that the circumstances remained the same, and individual commitment remained the same. The focus for the search would remain in the Exeter area. Nothing fundamental had changed; they all knew from personal experience that God was still in control and that He was worthy of their trust.

Fundraising continued, and in the period from September 2006 to April 2007 Rainbow Living raised £32,000. Members of the group signed up with local estate agents to receive details of potential properties. Less than a month had passed since the unsuccessful bid when another property came to their attention. It was viewed by members of the group, and again it seemed like it could work. An extract from the Rainbow Living Newsletter reads:

Since the last update a lot has happened, all for the good. After the disappointment of Barnfield Hill we regrouped, talked things through and prayed. Our friends and those interested in our project at church continued to support us and helped put things into perspective.

Some of us hit the Estate Agents in Exeter and got put on their mailing lists. Within a couple of days we had forwarded to us the details of a potential property in Exeter.

On paper the property had everything we were looking for. An advance party went ahead and viewed the house. They reported that all the signs were good and one Saturday morning the couple living in the house had a group of about 14 people viewing the house at the same time. I think it is fair to say that without exception all those that looked around the house liked it and felt it fitted the bill.

We had the property professionally valued and made the vendors an offer. After a little bit of negotiation we reached a mutually agreeable price which has been accepted.

The property will need re-wiring, plumbing being re-jigged, some structural adaptations to suit our needs. In addition to our bits and pieces a structural survey found that there is some remedial work needed on the annexe roof.

Suddenly things seemed to be falling into place; the vendors had accepted an offer from Rainbow Living for the property and could be out within six weeks. Most importantly, the Trust was happy to support the offer. A structural survey was carried out, and action points were raised. There was still a long way to go, but they were one step closer to realising their dream than they had been previously. The *is* needed dotting and the *ts* needed crossing, but the dream was fast becoming a reality!

Transforming the house into a home

Everyone was busy putting his or her skills to work so that the whole process could move forward. A list of jobs was drawn up, and detailed plans were put together with the associated costs. Insurances for the building and contents were negotiated. A solicitor completed the various searches and drew up a formal mortgage agreement. A bank account specifically for the house was opened. A local company – W.S. Atkins – offered their assistance in drawing up plans, particularly electrical and mechanical plans, and a local building firm – Rawle, Gammon and Baker – offered competitive rates on building materials, which the group was extremely grateful for.

Faith, hard work, patience, and perseverance were rewarded. Prayers were answered, and the culmination of so much energy reached a climax as Rainbow Living became the proud owners of their first property on 29 June 2007.

The Rainbow Living group gathered at the house that evening to celebrate this significant moment and to offer prayer and thanksgiving to God for His Faithfulness. An extract from the Rainbow Living newsletter reads:

What an exhilarating weekend! Friday passed seamlessly and Rainbow Living became the new owners of the property. I went down to the house late on Friday afternoon and had a few moments alone there with one other person. In a few quiet moments I had the chance to reflect on the long journey it had taken to get to this point.

I felt very emotional and an overwhelming sense that we had achieved the first, and very significant, step to improve and fashion the lives of our young people and those that might follow them. This building is the culmination of much work and effort by many, work and effort that involved ups and downs, joy and disappointments.

The moment passed quickly as the other Rainbow Living members arrived, including Sarah, Stephen and Joshua. Their excitement was tangible and catching. For many of us, including me, this was only the second time we had been inside the house. The house was every bit as good as I had remembered as we went from room to room checking everything out.

There was no time to rest on their laurels. Now that they owned the property Rainbow Living needed to make it into a home for the young people. The demolition process began, the whole group being consumed by the process.

Masses of material had to be removed from the property before the building phase could even begin. This work was carried out by volunteers and even taken away in their vehicles. More than 5,000 hours of work was given by volunteers to this project. This resulted in considerable sums of money being saved.

As ever, not all of the incidents were positive ones: as the parents and young people involved thought about their futures two of the young people felt unable to commit to the house. However, another young man stepped in who proved to be very enthusiastic about joining the venture and who was keenly supported by his parents. This didn't resolve the whole issue, though; it meant a situation of only four tenants, and three of them were male – not ideal for the one young lady who would be short of female company. There were also financial implications for the project. The loan repayments were based on the property being occupied by five tenants, and only having four would leave a significant shortfall in the payments. God was still in the equation, and at a later date one of the original young ladies decided she would join the others in the house.

Two unforeseen and expensive problems were identified: the third floor of the property needed new floor joists, and woodworm surfaced in parts of the house. Savings on the one hand were matched by unexpected expenditure on the other. It was beginning to feel like a rollercoaster ride.

Prospects began the recruitment process and launched a job fair at a church in the city. A prerequisite for the staff was that they had a Christian faith; obviously the staff who supported the young people in the house would have a significant impact on the success of the venture. All those involved felt that the commonality of a shared faith would help establish the house on a secure footing. The launch saw seven people express an interest in care support jobs. However, Prospects would need about twenty people in total to deliver the care with a mixture of full-time and part-time positions. This would mean a delay in the young people moving in. Prospects continued their discussions with Devon Adult Community Services over final care costs, but their lack of agreement resulted in ongoing anxiety for the families. It was agreed that individual families would contact their own care managers to progress their cases.

Money continued to be an issue, and Rainbow Living faced a shortfall in the projected alteration costs.

Meetings continued, as did the work of volunteers, and the property was transformed from a house into a home. Regular discussions took place over a whole host of topics from kitchen fitting, colour schemes, and whether or not door closers would be required to rental calculations, council tax, composting, and water butts. Time crept on with 2007 turning to 2008. Finances came in, and care packages were agreed, and finally on 16 June 2008 the five young people moved into the house.

Volunteers help transform the house.

A useable kitchen is created and is soon in use.

The back of the house is opened up with doors onto a patio area and wheelchair ramp for access into the garden.

A new beginning

It was an emotional time for all involved as the young people took their first steps towards independent living, and the parents coped with the "hole" left behind in their homes. It was a time of celebration, as those seeds of hope had brought forth the fruit in God's time, but it was also a time of huge adjustment that was not easy for those involved. The structure and routine of the new days needed to be established, and every individual involved had huge adjustments to make. For the parents it was difficult enough, but those with special needs had even more to contend with. Still certain that the vision was from God, and yet left with a tension as those adjustments took place, another extract from the Rainbow Living Newsletter encapsulates this dilema:

What I was not really prepared for were my feelings. I knew it would be difficult but I did not expect to miss him so much and found myself welling up on several occasions. It wasn't an easy week. Another parent, talking about their situation, summed it up pretty well - "I miss him dreadfully but I do not miss the caring" (the physical and emotional toll providing personal care).

There are mixed fortunes with the others, some doing well, some not doing so well. They all need your prayers and thoughts that they continue to cope with the changes …

Prospects now have a full complement of staff and they are a terrific bunch. They are getting to know the five and their little foibles, they are developing routines and activities. It is early days and a few things have to be sorted out and put in place but so far it is very encouraging. The Christianity of the staff shines through and delivers exactly what we as parents wanted. There is a tangible Christian ethos in the house from the simplicity of saying grace at the table, Christian music playing and worship sessions together.

Having cleared that massive hurdle there was no sitting back feeling satisfied. Rainbow Living as a charity was just beginning. A Retreat Day was booked for July, so that those involved would have opportunity to pray, meditate, praise God, and reflect on their vision for the future. Just because their own offspring had been given the opportunity to move forward the intention was never self-serving. The desire was to provide the opportunity for anyone who wanted to benefit from such an arrangement. God's faithfulness and His blessings were not something to be held on to; rather they were things that had been freely given and therefore should be shared.

Obviously the charity still had work to do in the oversight and management of the property that they had purchased, but that did not stop them from looking forward to extend their work. The Rainbow House became established, and everyone began to find his or her feet:

Over 3 months have gone by since the five young people moved in. I am delighted to report that it is a happy house and that our five youngsters are being looked after with great love and care by a staff who wear their Christianity on their sleeves. The five are happy, we are happy, Prospects are happy, Devon Adult and Community Services seem to be happy, and the partnership is working.

The carers are getting to know the five well and establishing meaningful bonds, some of which I venture to say will go beyond those of carer and client. There have been a few hiccups on the way but they have been successfully dealt with as individual's personalities and traits are better understood.

Staff have gradually found out what each of the five enjoy doing and have been able to source many of those activities locally. Of course there have had to be some compromises but that is life.

As a parent we have never been made to feel as though we are in the way, quite the contrary, our presence at the house always seems welcome by the staff and the five. It's no mean feat for the staff to have to cope with 10 parents who seem to turn up more *or less at any time and are still clucking over their charges but they have coped and they have done it well.*

As with anything in life things do change; Rainbow Living and Prospects have continued to address those changing needs through discussion and by working together. Life isn't perfect, but what they have found is quite unique – these young people have the opportunity to reach their God-given potential in a way that wouldn't have been possible if they had stayed at home with their parents. Their second project in Torquay is now complete, and another group with disabilities have been provided with housing and support: where the colours of the rainbow can reflect the beauty of God.

A tranquil garden to relax and enjoy the wonder of God's creation}

Rainbow Living

Rainbow Living is a charity (registered charity number 1116067) based on a Christian ethos. The charity seeks to provide accommodation and support for people with disability, particularly learning disability.

Mission statement

We value people with disability, particularly learning disability, and believe that they should be allowed to exercise choice in their own lives and that those choices should include where and with whom they live.

In pursuit of the above, Rainbow Living's aim is: The acquisition and ownership of property to house people with disability, particularly learning disability.

Our property will provide:

- Long term accommodation and security
- Homes that will give people continuity and stability in their lives
- Support and occupational opportunities

Rainbow Living will achieve this through the following goals:

- Short-term objective – to locate, purchase, and become the landlord of a house for five young adults with learning disability
- Medium Term objective – to locate, purchase, and become the landlord of additional houses for people with disability, particularly learning disability
- Long Term objective – to locate and purchase property where meaningful occupational, respite day care facilities, and holiday accommodation could be located for persons with disability, particularly learning disability

<u>Equal Opportunities</u>

Rainbow Living will not restrict the use of any property, or facilities, belonging to the charity, by persons wishing to live in or use our property or use our facilities on the grounds of the following:

- gender
- race
- severity of disability
- belief(s) held

However, Rainbow Living, as the landlord and in conjunction with our care provider, will consider how a potential service user may impact on others already participating in an existing project.

To find out more:

www.rainbowliving.org.uk

Alternatively, contact them via Facebook or Twitter.

Having begun the process of writing this account Rainbow Living has, as a charity, continued to flourish. Their second property in the Torbay area has been completely refurbished, allowing an additional group of disabled adults to live a more independent life through the provision of housing and support. A third home is currently being investigated, and the aspiration for the long term plans are very much alive. I am certain that in the not too distant future God's blessing will be evident through the provision of further accommodation and a rural therapeutic community with meaningful occupation and accommodation. Those who are so often marginalized by our society can be valued and have the opportunity to live full and productive lives; as Rainbow Living grows so more and more people will benefit from their work.

About the author

Tracey has spent her career in education, teaching and supporting young people. She has a particular interest in special needs and has worked extensively with both challenging and vulnerable young people. Her Christian faith motivates her to reach out, particularly to those who are marginalised by society. Finding out more about this special group has been an inspiration, and she wants to encourage others to see the potential in every God-given life.

Lightning Source UK Ltd.
Milton Keynes UK
UKOW05f0819181114

241767UK00002B/158/P